Queer Physics

Queer Physics

Poems by

David Southward

© 2025 David Southward. All rights reserved.
This material may not be reproduced in any form, published,
reprinted, recorded, performed, broadcast,
rewritten, or redistributed without
the explicit permission of David Southward.
All such actions are strictly prohibited by law.

Cover design by Shay Culligan
Cover image by Gary Meulemans on Unsplash
Author photo by David Southward

ISBN: 978-1-63980-894-6
Library of Congress Control Number: 2025943309

Kelsay Books
502 South 1040 East, A-119
American Fork, Utah 84003
Kelsaybooks.com

Acknowledgments

Thanks to the editors of the journals, anthologies, and websites in which the following poems first appeared:

Able Muse: "Office Hours"
Alabama Literary Review: "Sunday at the Carpet Emporium," "Mornings with Sammy," "Staying at Dad's," "Swimming in Walden Pond," "Tree Swallows," "What He Saw in the River"
Blotterature: "Dirty Energy"
Bramble: "Love Keeps Coming," "1981"
The Classical Outlook: "Sappho at the Beach"
Frost Farm Prize for Metrical Poetry: "Mary's Visit" (2019 Winner)
Gyroscope Review: "William Shakespeare"
Light: "Mystery Solved," "Thinness Makes Us Cruel," "Song of the Bog"
Maria W. Faust Sonnet Contest Winners: "1984" (2022 Regional Winner), "On the Death of a Journalist at 44" (2023 Regional Winner), "Black Ice" (2024 Laureates' Choice)
Measure: "Trench Art," "The Dowager's Egg"
Moss Piglet: "Viking"
Naugatuck River Review: "Laughing with Alice" (2023 Contest Finalist)
Orchards Poetry Review: "Truth in the Midlands"
Poetry by the Sea: "An Aging Poet Explains" (2021 Kim Bridgford Memorial Sonnet Contest Winner)
Razor Lit Mag: "Pablo and Gertrude"
Sixfold: "The First Tattoo," "Object Lesson," "Boiling Point 2020," "The Pelican"
THINK Journal: "Out of the Labyrinth," "Channel Crosser," "1972," "1974," "1977," "Storm Windows," "William Morris"
Third Wednesday: "Ferns"
Wisconsin Fellowship of Poets Calendar: "River Men"
Wisconsin People & Ideas: "Saint Simone" (2nd Place, 2021 Poetry Contest), "Notes Toward a Queer Physics"

Contents

1. Half-Hour Magic

1971	15
1972	16
Mary's Visit	17
The Dowager's Egg	19
Sunday at the Carpet Emporium	20
The Dog Walkers	22
Song of the Bog	23
Swimming in Walden Pond	24
Office Hours	25

2. What We Do to Ourselves

1974	29
1975	30
The Preparation	31
William Morris	33
Hopper's People	35
Tie-Up on Pewaukee Lake	37
Party Killer	39
Mystery Solved	41
Thinness Makes Us Cruel	42
On the Death of a Journalist at 44	43
Object Lesson	44
At Housman's Grave	45
The First Tattoo	46

3. Spies Who Love Us

1976	51
1977	52
1977	53
Mother	54
Mornings with Sammy	55
River Men	57
Channel Crosser	58
Pablo and Gertrude	60
Trans Friend	61
Truth in the Midlands	62
At Tuckpoint	64

4. Bullets and Bracelets

1978	67
1979	68
Dirty Energy	69
Boiling Point 2020	71
Trench Art	74
Viking	75
Storm Windows	77
Black Ice	78
You Scream I Scream	79
Saint Simone	81

5. Beauty's Mark

1981	85
1983	86
Out of the Labyrinth	87
Sappho at the Beach	94
William Shakespeare	96
What He Saw in the River	97
Tree Swallows	98
Natural Wonder	100

6. Queer Physics

1983	105
1984	106
1985	107
Notes Toward a Queer Physics	108
Staying at Dad's	110
A 20th-Century Scrapbook	111
Ghost Tour	113
The Pelican	114
Laughing with Alice	115
An Aging Poet Explains	117
Ferns	118
Love Keeps Coming	119

1. Half-Hour Magic

1971

The first mystery: how was a boy, at three,
jolted from intuition's babbling stream
by curvy forms and drumbeats on TV—
before he'd learned to call his waking dream
Josie and the Pussycats?
                              I'm back
reliving it—the almost funny way
a hairstyle spectrum, blonde to red to black,
comes into focus; how the bandmates play
barelegged, in skintight leopard leotards;
how, as their theme song starts, a bolt of joy
goes through me that so thoroughly bombards
my circuits, I catch fire—not quite the boy
I was. And that's the second mystery:
what do we call the Pussycat in me?

1972

While Mom gets dressed for nursing school, I drown
in *That Girl:* Ann, the bubbly debutante
whose chocolate eyes and waterfall bouffant
draw men like flies. In white gloves, skipping down
Park Avenue, she's late for a rehearsal,
yet squints to look up through Manhattan's glare
(cuing the bebop soundtrack's sax and snare)
and sees herself—projected, universal—
a dream girl who's part woman and part child.
Her boyfriend, smitten by the scratch and squeak
of "Donald!" in his ear, waits for her kisses
like Echo for the budding of Narcissus.
Pretending I'm the one that she's beguiled,
I rub her phantom lipstick from my cheek.

Mary's Visit

We watched her car pass slowly by our house
and circle back with purpose. It appeared
she'd spotted us, nestled in our dream
of a stone cottage from an earlier time.
She parked out front and asked to come inside.
Naturally we concluded she was lost

or peddling religion. All she had lost
however, was certainty: could this house
have been her Great Aunt Gertrude's? "Look inside
if you want," we told her. Something might appear
to bring back vanished memories of the time
she played here with her siblings. "I've had dreams,"

she said, "of finding it again"—one dream
in which the porch was sloped like ours. Half lost
in the wistful currents pulling her through time,
I pictured the aunt living in our house—
and how, whenever relatives appeared
on the doorstep, she'd hold the pain inside

her knotted joints, and smile. Here inside
our damp, shade-darkened rooms, her niece would dream
that Gertrude was a witch, that ghosts appeared
behind the bathtub curtain, and that lost
in the woods out back of the spinster's house
were her missing children. This stored-up time

had become a burden to our guest, a time
that had no place. It rattled around inside,
where doubts began to creep: although our house
looked like the one she'd come to in her dream,
its lines were off; the floor plan did not match
a pattern that had all but disappeared.

"Maybe"—she tapped her head—"it's all up here."
One's memories grew entangled over time
with longing, hope, regret. The thread's soon lost
that leads out of the maze we live inside—
bumping against the glass doors of our dreams
in search of some distinct, authentic house.

Her fear appeared to change the mood inside
as time resumed its course. Clutching her dream
of what she'd lost, Mary left our house.

The Dowager's Egg

Some gasp to see this pink and gold surprise
enshrined within a bulletproof display.
Diamonds and pearls enlace its patterned sides
with beadwork from the House of Fabergé.
The toy it held (now lost, the guidebooks say)
was a miniature sedan—with Catherine the Great
perched inside—and serfs to bear her weight.

A gift for the widowed mother of the Tsar,
it blazed for her that Easter in '14
from a clawfoot stand, beside the samovar.
Enthralled to find its hidden figurine,
she thought of how her husband had foreseen
disaster for their pampered boy. Yet here,
as she held the egg up to the chandelier

and turned it, glory speckled her peignoir.
No glimmer of concern; no flash of fate
strafing an Archduke's ornamented car;
no rumors that her son would abdicate
or, worse, fall victim to some newborn state.
No, what she saw was pure: the artifact
with all of its surprises still intact.

Sunday at the Carpet Emporium

The showroom walls of Shabahang & Sons
shimmer with rugs: prismatic tapestries
whose dyed-wool hues and petaloid designs
serve as a backdrop for the heir, Behzad,
to ply his trade. Sporting a merchant's smile,
he greets us with a manicured handshake
and summons an assistant with his eyes.
"Functional works of art," he deems his rugs,
beseeching us to feel one's thickened pile
brushing our palm-flesh like a camel's hide—
to rub our hands across its matted nap
and watch for dark reversals in the sheen.
He points his helper to a waist-high stack
of tribal 6 x 9s, at the ends of which
the two men stand—turning rugs like pages
of an ancient manuscript. In perfect sync
they grip the corners, peel the fabrics back
to reveal, slice by slice, a Persian fruit
as fathomless in its geometry
as if it were the sum of one's own life.
"You like?" Behzad pauses, noting our taste
for saffron twined through blues and burgundies.
"Go on," we urge. We want to see the whole
of his inventory; we won't be satisfied
until the last persimmon leaf is flipped.

Flipping the last, the men start turning back
the inventory, firmly satisfied
we want to splurge. They know how far we'll go
sorting through blues and twining burgundies
before we pause. "You liked this," notes Behzad,
tapping our rug of choice—the sum of life
fathomed in its geometric play;
a slice of Persia densely veined, like fruit
peeled in a back corner of paradise.
We sink our hands in its plush manuscript:
a page on which two men might stand or turn
their chairs at the end of a tribal 9-to-6—
their china stacked with helpings, points well made
or meeting with reversals in the dark.
We rub our eyes: across this matted land
where camels never ride, nor palm fronds brush
beseechingly one's pile of thickened dreams,
can a rug redeem? The function, the work of art
is a summoning of vistas like the sky's—
its handsome greeting, one of many cures.
The sport of trade, the smile of merchandise
serves Behzad, who drops back in thin air;
as wooly petals ply their dyed designs,
our shimmery Mastercard's prismatic chip
suns the showroom walls of Shabahang.

The Dog Walkers

I watch them from a window at the gym:
his coltish Boxer, eager to explore
the hind-parts of her Golden Labrador,
strains at the harness, pulling with such vim
the poor guy's hauled into a tug-of-war—
as if the Boxer now were walking him
in circles around the Lab. With leg and limb
caught between spiraling leashes, soon all four
are tangled in desire's warp and woof.
He looks embarrassed, kneeling to unweave
the damage. But she laughs! His Boxer's goof
has won her over; both act less aloof;
and while the dogs, well sniffed, make signs to leave,
she rattles off a number to retrieve.

Song of the Bog

Studies have shown that female frogs,
   listening for the song
of wooing males, get most turned on
   by an absurdly long

tune drawn out—or one that's short,
   compact and repetitious.
Either approach will wow a mate,
   provided it's ambitious.

Isn't this eerily like the choice
   between heroic verse
that rumbles on, and lyric rhyme
   whose lovesick cries are terse?

Some nights Homer's scrolling tongue
   extends to suck us in;
on others, lonely Petrarch's peep
   gets under our damp skin.

Narration, pumped with metaphors
   by bards grown fat on war,
may fascinate—but the heart leaps
   for a pond-scum troubadour

who might just be our secret prince!
   What gene pool would prohibit
our passing up an epic croak
   for lyric's ribbit-ribbit?

Swimming in Walden Pond

My suitemate at the conference rapped my door
at five a.m. Through darkened streets we ran
in trunks and T-shirts, allied in our plan
to beat the tour groups. This was '94

yet I still see the clearing through the trees:
its granite glint, a mirror to the sky.
A crow's caw scours the beach as Tom and I
wade into Walden's stillness by degrees

till a last plunge swashes its cold caress
against our necks. Hushed voices—all we know
of Alcotts, Hawthornes, Emersons, Thoreau—
swirl through our fingers. Steeped in sacredness,

we try not to disturb the moment's power;
our circling pathways ripple and converge
while, through the pines, we watch the sun emerge
with its full blaze intact. For half an hour

we drank that sunshine, as our bodies drew
inscriptions on the slick of its white beam,
knowing too well our dream, like any dream,
would end soon. Gooseflesh drying, what to do

but brush sand from our feet, pull on our socks,
run back to Concord? Chilled and soggy-toed
we hugged the shoulder, passing on the road
a school bus—slowing, sighing like an ox.

Office Hours

Plato must have known what it was like:
the handsome freshman wrestling with a text
whose point escapes him. Flustered and perplexed,
he comes to you for help. A pleasant spike
of interest rouses you from your routine;
you note his solid build, the swimmer's thighs,
the look of trepidation in blue eyes
adjusting to a realm of things unseen.
Guiding him through its fog, like Socrates
you watch the light of comprehension come
quivering into his mind—a soundless thrum
distinct as starlight breaking through the trees.
Grateful, he zips his backpack, nods goodbye,
and leaves you to the mercy of the sky.

2. What We Do to Ourselves

1974

For Christmas, all my wishes are fulfilled:
Malibu Barbie, Ken, their luxe RV.
From Dad's unease, I sense that he's not thrilled—
but nothing's going to blunt my ecstasy
at handling these forbidden figurines.
I love their graceful poses, plastic smell,
the way my mind heats up with lurid scenes
not pitched in any boardroom at Mattel.
On a dark beach, Barbie and her man
pledge love before their god on rubber knees
while bandits, crouching, eye their caravan
from the dense shadows of surrounding trees.
When boys ask me to play, I'll leave inside
this outlaw Barbie world it's best to hide.

1975

I piece together verses of a song:
a girl whose horse runs off succumbs to fever
calling him—"Wildfire!"—all night long
in a fierce storm. Our Pioneer receiver
reveals a power I didn't know it had—
to thrash with snow the dark Nebraskan plains;
to drive a pony from its stable—mad
for one whose scent he knows to take his reins.
I am the horse, the girl, and dying farmer
who tells her story, hoping one last freeze
will reunite them. Stripped of mortal armor,
we ride on Wildfire through brittle trees—
blinded by tears too hot to be withstood,
in disbelief that sadness feels this good.

The Preparation

Tubes in your mouth and wrists. What little life
trickles through your bloodstream makes us think
of the proud daughter, sister, mother, wife

who swallowed back her sadness, drink by drink.
Like cargo on a life raft cast adrift,
your body undulates; you rise and sink

as airflow through the mattress gently shifts
and stimulates your limbs—a timed regime
to keep you battle-ready. Bearing gifts,

we call your name to wake you from a dream
you've spent three weeks in. Presently a nurse
and techs barge in and, like a racecar team,

convert your bed into a sort of hearse
to roll you to the lab for an MRI.
Doctors, concerned your mind fares even worse

than your organs, warn your husband to stand by,
but not to speculate or look for hope
in a finger's spasm or fluttering of an eye.

"Is she wearing metal?" they ask. He mumbles, "Nope"—
then remembers seeing a pair of tiny earrings
buried in your hair. Retracing the slope

from neck to ear, he feels for engineering
behind your lobe and pinches at the core
to release it. The companion, disappearing

somewhere in your bedsheets long before,
is nowhere to be found. With a helpless sigh
he watches them wheel you down the corridor,

wondering to himself why he can't cry—
or curse, let go, scream out, forgive, condemn—
anything but this bland, drawn-out goodbye

of waiting. But instead, through the a.m.,
he'll sit here—turning over in his hand
the last of your defenses, clasp and stem.

William Morris

I built my love a red brick house—
and watched her pace the floors
as if to say
"I've lost my way."
Thinking she missed the verdant woods,
I brought the woods indoors:

trellises, interlaced with vines,
to hide a bare bleak wall;
thick-sewn drapes
cartooned with shapes
of bird and leaf and flower—to mime
creation's ceaseless scrawl.

I learned to mold and solder lead,
brush glass with rainbow dye.
Hand in glove
I cast my love
a window, where a knight and queen
fused under ruby sky.

My love, grown paler, gently wept.
I carved for her a bed
of cunning form—
and kept her warm
with goose down, gathered into quilts
of homespun woolen thread.

Unease possessed me. I wrote lectures,
preached to working men
on craft and trade:

how goods well made
with loving hands would make Britannia
beautiful again.

Yet love? Unyielding. Crushed at heart,
I limped on in my quest
like one half-blind—
a fool, to find
this furnishing of paradise
would never let me rest.

Hopper's People

They stare into coffee cups, or gaze at wheat
from windows with imaginary glass.
They fixate on the smoothness of a street.
An introspective class
from dusk to night,
they ponder how they might have got things right.

We're drawn to their abstraction by a hope
they seem to share—that selves can be renewed.
The fresh identity toward which they grope
in contemplative moods
can still be seen
in hues of rose and phosphorescent green.

But look too long, and you might say defeat
has cornered them. Like dollhouse props
their furniture is kept too clean, too neat.
No accidental drops
of paint or sweat
will rouse them from their theater of regret.

Meanwhile, sunbeam diamonds cross the floor
as shadows in the doorways turn pure black.
Motel room, diner, office, general store
prepare for an attack
of twilight blues.
A voice inside the head throbs, *Choose. Choose.*

The news from Hopper's people is that souls
are faceted and feral. Hard as we strive
to settle into human pigeonholes,

old instincts come alive
when evening has filled
our senses with a wilderness we've stilled.

Tie-Up on Pewaukee Lake

I watch you, Matthew, hop aboard a boat
that's hitched to this you've left me standing in—
in disbelief at how friends float
away from sorrowful disclosures

that interrupt their weekend recreation.
Your sister's husband, finishing his chores
early, it seems—with a worried grin
she'd never seen before—collapsed

sideways on their disinfected floor
to die at forty-two. A loss too vast
to comprehend, their swift divorce
has made you philosophical—

why else would you have dropped your eyes to ask
whether we gay men undermine our role
as spouses, when we don our mask
of leisure sports in mid-July?

Watching you slip, unanswered, into droll
horseplay on a snug pontoon, I try
to see our situation whole.
Couples: straddling middle age

with barefoot ease, no moping kids nearby
to nudge us toward that platonic stage
of marriage. What makes you and I
reluctant in our revelry?

We sense how partners slyly disengage;
each dallies with the thought of being free

to trace another man's ribcage
or try the bittersweet cologne

of muscle pressed against upholstery.
Behavior we would normally disown
is legal here; a canopy
shades our embarrassed eyes, as nude

flesh beneath a swimsuit's peel is shown.
The shredded-lime-and-vodka-tinted mood
that mellows our accustomed tone
and cloaks in a euphoric haze

this stalled armada: is it for our good?
The air's so hot, I'd like to rinse the glaze
of sweat and sunscreen I exude
in the lake my man's been lounging in—

too far away for me to read his eyes.
He's with the pack that's drifted off . . . till someone
sober calls them back: the strays
who sigh and kick and kick and kick.

Party Killer

"Have I shown you the owl?" asks our host,
filling our highballs with ice.
He towels his hands, unlocks his phone,
assures us that his mind was blown
to catch it on film and, like a boast,
hands us his device.

It's shocking, the close-up frontal shot.
A hunched god fills the frame—
the yellow rims of its outraged eyes,
plumage tensing with surprise,
recall how the flash blazed so hot
it set the pines aflame.

"Look," he says, and with finger and thumb
zooms in on the featherettes
that frame the creature's oval face
in layered fans, like fraying lace—
until their winnowed silks become
clean fishbones. One forgets

how decorous nature is, how stark
its costume of attack.
The pointing of a widow's peak
toward the scissors of a beak
is like some herald in the dark
that won't be answered back.

For hours I imitate the drawl
of small talk, as faces pass.
Stabbing my toothpick into cheese,

I chew on news and pleasantries
while, over a shoulder, seeing all
reflected in black glass.

Mystery Solved

They showed up daily on the news:
human feet, still in their shoes,
found on a coastline—quite alone
and severed at the anklebone.

Who were their owners? What cruel joke
was played on the truncated folk?
Had they been victims of a shark?
A psychopath's revolting lark?

The thought of litter so horrific
made the seaside less pacific.
Attendance at the beaches slumped.
Police admitted: they were stumped.

Until the lucky day, that is,
a diligent forensic wiz,
by studying the ocean's tides,
retraced the paths of *suicides*

who'd leapt from bridges miles away
and drifted . . . to become the prey
of hungry fish (who somehow knew
that Nikes weren't worth chewing through).

It's strange: although these souls gave in,
their shoes proved tougher than their skin.
The spring with which all hope was hurled
kept one foot planted in this world.

Thinness Makes Us Cruel

The newly slim are never rid
of fat they carried as a kid;
the discipline it took to lose,
the bathroom-scale-and-mirror blues.
Shame's loose clothes leave residues
of failure even in success—
with moody bouts of vengefulness.

Observe, when they forgo dessert,
how long they eye it (as though hurt
by those who nibble, laugh, and chatter
with zero fear of growing fatter).
Clinging to thinness like an adder,
they'll wave goodnight, unsatisfied,
and gnaw the eggshell of their pride.

Such veterans of self-denial
assume that thinness is a trial,
with love as its deserved reward.
But love obeys a different lord.
It comes for those who drop their sword—
who'll traipse through undefended lands
eating from its open hands.

And so the thin re-stock their shelves
with canned reflections of themselves,
remembering how long it's been
since they were able to dig in.
There's still a chance—if by some sin
they violate their golden rule
of non-indulgence—they'll begin
to realize: thinness makes us cruel.

On the Death of a Journalist at 44

I see him in my classroom at eighteen—
sullen and sneering, ready to attack
the princess, suck-up, jock, or lit-mag hack—
his heart like tinder doused in gasoline.

Confronting him, I saw a young James Dean
let down his guard—admit to his own lack
of gracefulness at holding anger back,
with no one by his side to intervene.

I wasn't there to see his hard-earned rise
through journalism's ranks; his wedding day;
the flutter of his firstborn's trusting eyes—

or how, as fog rolled in one wintry day,
the loneliness of trying to be good
encircled the last bridge on which he stood.

Object Lesson

Much as I failed
    to grasp it at the time,
my threadbare silk
    security blanket
must have posed a threat
    (however veiled) to Dad
that snow-piled night
    in the Midwest, when Cronkite
veered from an oil crisis
    to a solar eclipse
while Mom laid the table.
    Dad snatched
the fistful of rag
    from my hand—
flashing that big-brotherly
    half sneer, half smile
I knew meant trouble—
    and opened the front door
to throw it
    to the howling weather.
I wailed, ran
    straight into the maelstrom
to save my blankie. And maybe
    that was all
Dad needed to see: a spark
    of opposition, his only son
demanding love—knowing
    how hard it was
to come by that year,
    how little there was
between him and me
    and the ice.

At Housman's Grave

Alfred, I was born like you:
a boy aloof from other boys.
Afraid my love might show, I too
perfected a veneer of poise.

I gave my heart to one as young;
when the time came to take it back,
I didn't complain. I held my tongue,
adjusted to a tightened rack

and learned, like you, to see through pain.
Soldiers in their trench at night
can make out stars, however vain
the prospect of such far-off light.

Trying to match your stoic ways,
I bit my tongue almost in two.
Now, though my whole affection stays,
it's time that I let go of you—

tip my cap and say farewell.
Writing more open-hearted songs,
I'll break the melancholic spell
that's held me back. I'll right old wrongs,

and for some lad I'll leave this coin:
a sign of friendship only found
up here—before we, too, must join
you lonesome fellows underground.

The First Tattoo

My whole life I've been afraid
    to stain my body, insisting
no mark is meaningful enough
    for ink's permanence. Still here
I find myself: sitting backwards
    in Aaron's chair, as he engraves
palm fronds on my scapula. A gift
    from my husband—to mark
the threshold of my fiftieth year:
    palms trees and grackles, a Gulf Coast
childhood tinged by adults-only
    Mexican getaways. With six hours
to kill, I'm nose-deep in a hardback
    memoir (Springsteen's) as massive
as *Moby-Dick*. Eyeballs distracted
    by Aaron's pin-ups of arabesque
biceps, I think of Queequeg,
    the Pequod's nude harpooner,
stunning Ishmael with his aboriginal
    tattoo-treatise on the universe
no longer legible; and how, in college,
    I winced at the keloidal make-up
of Maori warriors—irritated with ash
    to highlight youth's passage
into pain, warfare, marriage, labor.
    It taught me how history could live
under the skin—indelible yet invisible
    until teased out with a stylus.
Like in last week's episode of *Nova*
    on the tattoo's origin: fresh evidence
of ochre and charcoal pulverized
    a hundred thousand years ago

by Homo sapiens rounding the Cape
    of Good Hope. (From the same cave
came Earth's first graffiti, a crayon-
    red hashtag on a granite slab—
our meaty brain already impatient
    to make something of itself.)
As Aaron's needle probes the V-
    shaped convergence of palm-trunks, I
almost faint; this vertebral crux
    is my tattoo's darkest part. I squint
to refocus on the open book, Springsteen
    guiding followers into the crevasse
of his depression—no more the Boss
    than Ahab was captain on the trail
of a lost leg; than I was, all those years
    I didn't write, fearing the itch
of the past like a wound too buried
    to be scratchable. Not until
Aaron smears my scars with aloe gel
    and hands me a mirror, do I see
all that's behind me. Like the Boss says:
    we're born to run. No wonder we need
such painful, beautiful reminders
    of what we can do to ourselves.

3. Spies Who Love Us

1976

Kojak, SWAT, Beretta, Starsky & Hutch—
into this hardnosed underworld of grime
come Charlie's Angels: blow-dried, more in touch
with civil, stylish ways to sniff out crime.
Watching them train, I sip a chocolate malt.
Though this will be the year that I get fat,
the Angels shrug: "A sweet tooth? Not your fault."
It's greed and lies and lust they bristle at.
Part of me wants to *be* them: toned and slim,
the agent of a Zeus-like playboy's will—
but on my terms, untouchable by him
or any lord of earth. I'd have my fill
of being at once a tigress and a lamb.
Lapping up milk, accepting what I am.

1977

The passion that I share with Dad is Bond—
James Bond. He's suave yet rakish, stern but fair,
with confidence and style so far beyond
most men, I'd like to ask: What's *under* there?
Summer rolls out his Lotus and tuxedo
in *The Spy Who Loved Me*. Floored, we watch (*No way!*)
the car turn sub—and launch its own torpedo—
as his snake-charm theme begins its brass sashay.
We know, before the end, that James will score
a babe. It's fun rehashing while we drive
who plays him better: Connery or Moore?
With windows down, the whole night feels alive—
as if the stars flickering high above me
are sending signals out to spies who'll love me.

1977

Reading in my back yard, I'm Nancy Drew.
At brunch with Ned; out driving; making time
to shine a flashlight on the web of crime
behind an old credenza. Oh, it's true
my hammock's sinking, stretched from fence to tree,
and nothing but a blotted paper plate
remains of cherry pop tarts I just ate,
but Nancy doesn't judge or hassle me.
She's too intent on seeing life's whole truth
with stoic grace—a worldliness and poise
that makes those corn-fed pups, the Hardy Boys,
seem boring. Nestled with a female sleuth,
I feel more at home—a boy involved
in mysteries no man has ever solved.

Mother

A catcher's mitt that hugs your hand.
The imprint of a wedding band.

A perfume that you can't quite place.
Nasturtium blossoms in a vase.

The cool of grass beneath your feet.
The nibbling of a parakeet.

A walk on autumn's clearest night.
A window of galactic light—

and in the window's glass, a trace
of flickers from a fireplace.

Mornings with Sammy

He used to barrel out the sliding door,
careen across the deck, vault and soar
over the steps to crash at the maple's feet.
He'd lunge toward its boughs—as if to eat
the squirrels who paced the branching world above.
Sniffing the ground-scents like a drunk in love,
he'd track each odor to its source and lick it—
then bound into the border garden's thicket,
his white tail whisking hostas, ferns, and mint
like a fur tornado. Anxiously, we'd squint
to watch him slalom through our lily wands,
drape slobber on the rhubarb's giant fronds,
or brave the rosebush, thorny hackles raised.
Sternly I'd call his name; he'd look back, dazed
for a moment. But noticing how sparrows
alighted from the sky like hostile arrows,
he'd spring to action—chase them off the fence,
start barking with a clownlike vehemence—
as if to show me no work was so hard
as proving oneself master of one's yard.

These days his routine is more sedate.
He'll breakfast, nap till seven (maybe eight),
slide off the couch and glance up, mucus-eyed,
to let us know he'll have a look outside.
A few steps past the threshold, there's a pause.
He sniffs the air. Nostrils tensed, he draws
decaying fumes of everything that grows
into the laboratory of his nose,
sifting the wind for signs of fresh turf wars
with ears blown back like little semaphores.
There's no more need to trample leaf or limb.

Now the garden's treasures come to him—
sensations once so hurried and erratic
becoming denser, marbled and chromatic.
It's comforting to watch our grizzled scout
stand rigid on the deck, almost devout,
savoring—like a book too good to last—
the stirred-up fragrances of summers past.

River Men

They steer the rafts; they stow the gear;
they brave the rapids year by year,
beloved by all whose lives depend
upon the skills of river men.

To sleep with one eye on the raft
and guard the rations, fore and aft,
is crucial in the hinterland.
It takes a steady river man.

They hold their tongues when guests complain
about the clouds, the cold, the rain—
knowing one does not offend
the gallant code of river men.

With camp set up, their day near done,
they'll work in cheerful unison
to feed their floating caravan
the supper of a river man.

They show us how to meet duress
with absolute preparedness.
For who knows what comes round the bend?
Be ready, like the river men.

Channel Crosser

What if the London painter John Millais
had gone to Giverny to meet Monet,
in hopes of fusing England's straitlaced style
with French aesthetics, down to les détails?

And say that Claude, a grizzle-bearded man,
leads John across the bridge in his jardin,
famed for its pictorial lily swamp.
In purple-blossomed billows, le printemps

surrounds the shaded grasses where they lay
a blanket for their picnic déjeuner—
hearing, amid the bower's fragrant hues,
the love-chirps of a feathery chanteuse.

"I've come because I want to learn," says John,
"the secret of your—what's the word? Élan?
You Paris chaps are all the rage abroad,
like bicycles and absinthe. Tell me, Claude,

how does one's paintbrush conjure like a wand
such landscapes to awaken le beau monde?
Might a Victorian hope to raise the bar
of public taste, importing l'art pour l'art?"

Squinting into the distant midday glare
at lovely forms emerging en plein air,
Claude swirls, as wild geese serenely honk,
an effervescent quaff of cool vin blanc

and answers, "Bien sûr! (Here, try the leeks.)
But first you must give up your idée fixe
that pictures should have meaning. If I may:
what meaning has that willow, s'il vous plaît?

Success in art is won by those who dare
to wield a brush with nature's laissez faire.
Her brazen beauty proves that even God
takes pleasure in creation's sweet façade."

The clack of spoons in empty pots de crème
conceals an awkward hint in John's "Ahem."
His instincts warn there's something not quite pure
about his host's insouciant hauteur:

for all that dashing style and French finesse,
the eye for color, infinite tendresse
and savoir faire, a bloke could go too far
indulging pleasure like some bête noire.

Claude, with drooping eyes, begins to sway
while John shoos flies away from the pâté
wondering: should an artist curb his yen
to moralize life's jumbled mise-en-scène?

We'll leave him there—seeking a middle way,
neither uptight nor shallow (nor outré),
to please both avant-garde and bourgeoisie—
bridging two realms with English jeu d'esprit.

Pablo and Gertrude

she is all ears for his theories of the nude
while pacing the studio others have no patience;

absorbing each word only Gertrude
a fellow diablo appears to understand

shapes so defiantly yearning to be skewed
with eyes aglow and sex contorted

she finds his rhythms like a dissonant étude
bracingly apropos (if somewhat more

amusing for being offensive to a prude)
plucked from the nouveau her queer poetry, too,

and muscular womanhood must be viewed
like fruit sur la table— from all angles;

in such prisms through such plenitude
possibilities grow the mind gathers

toward a realization how little is understood
of the great *Silencio!* between two people

where truths converge; an artist's misconstrued
this is why she goes because he sees

Trans Friend

He says to us—
no, *she* says

get used to it.
He's always—Jesus,

she's always
been this way

inside, where it counts.
Wherever we thought

he used to be,
she was. See?

It's easy, so stop
overthinking—just

make the swap
inside, where it counts.

Wherever you thought
him, his, he,

she was. She is.
She will be.

Truth in the Midlands

A scattered flock
of English sheep
dines while standing
ankle deep
in rain-drenched grass
between the steep
chalk hills of Ilam,
where you and I
have come to walk.

Their bleats and brays,
nasal orations
affirmed by meek,
clicking rotations
of their jaws,
are like a conversation
overheard. It could be praise
for a god of sheep, or rain,
or frisky lambs

who wander off,
then skip and canter
back to their dam—
rubbing their hides
against her flank
as if they've only
her to thank.
Meanwhile,
in the steady drizzle,

you startle me
with a blunt appraisal
of my personality.
I'm *stealthy, suave,
controlled,* you say.
More cat than dog.
And yet the sheep
don't blink, or blush
or look away;

they watch me, bored,
through forelock mops—
like stoners camped
on mountaintops,
smoking till dawn.
To such contented
English sheep,
I'm one more secret
Earth can keep.

At Tuckpoint

for Roland Sardeson

Etched in stone, an aged man's face
juts forth as if it owns the place,
and from a distance almost smirks.
It's one of many limestone quirks

your life was filled with—now ours, too.
Whoever sleeps here thinks of you:
sorting through scrap to save what's good;
buffing planks of home-sawn wood;

comparing stone (amazed how light
brings out the spark in dolomite);
and fitting panes of colored glass
through which your boyhood memories pass.

Embedding marbles with your thumb
in thick, wet mortar, did you hum—
chuckling to think with what surprise
we'd find that Tuckpoint's walls have eyes?

Doorknobs, handrails, towel hooks, moldings
restored to wonder—precious holdings
tucking us in to bed each night.
We feel your stonework, friend. It's tight.

4. Bullets and Bracelets

1978

The strips of tinfoil curled around my wrists
are Wonder Woman's bracelets. I am ten.
Though other boys, I'm told, look up to men,
I chop the air with bullet-blocking fists
and twirl a lasso snipped from spooled jute.
My bathing suit shows off the chubby thighs
Dad calls "cherubic." (Shy in front of guys,
I camouflage my breasts.) My tube-sock boot
kickboxes lunkheads—henchmen of the foe
who's lured me to a showdown. Now we'll see
how vulnerable a heroine can be
and still prevail. Then everyone will know:
it's useless for a man to force his will
on Love, the mama's boy who's armed to kill.

1979

Snug in my Underoos, I'm Aquaman!
As the Han boys untie their swim trunks' lacings
and yank them down, I see by routine scan
their penises, like sausage links, have casings
that end in crinkly tips. What foul play,
I wonder, made their wieners look that way?
They tell me of a secret operation
performed on *me*—before I could consent.
When Mom confirms the tale, my mutilation
nags me. Thinking of what I underwent
in bed at night, I squirm and don't feel clean.
With skin still itching from the dried chlorine
I stretch my waistband—find where I was pruned
and left two-toned: an Aquaman marooned.

Dirty Energy

Can you feel it?
A burning, particulate
mist in the sinus;
vented plumes
of benzene, pyridine,
combustible hothouse
percolations blanketing
the biosphere; stray skeins
of rainbow coagula
speckling the backwash
of hydraulic fractures;
raw tissue—flensed
from panting gills, lungs.

The landscape's changed.
Wildlife reels
in a seismic typhoon
of offshore drills,
rash hopscotch
of shale beds—stripped
by tar-sand cartels,
methane billowing
from caulked spiracles.

The mixture's powerful:
chemical broths flushed
through porous bitumen;
embankments giving way;

toxin detectors ticking;
temperatures higher.

Doesn't it almost
exhilarate? That fizz
of carbonated rain—
the miracle of water
catching fire?

Boiling Point 2020

Dear Mike, news of your death finds me
on one of those days in July
when the sliding door opens

to a porridge of steam, and all of Wisconsin
takes shade. Slogging through Facebook,
I'd been pondering how to respond

to paranoid memes, shared by cousins
I barely know—insinuations
that COVID is a deep-state hoax,

that Blacks are racist too, that Emperor Trump
will rescue the nation
from godless conspiracy—when Dad calls

to report that you, retired doctor and father
of six, close friend of 45 years,
have braced a gun to the roof of your mouth

and left this world in a wreath of smoke.
A survivor of stroke, dragging one leg at 83
through God knows what humiliations,

maybe you faltered in Florida's sweltering heat,
or stopped noticing the horizon,
or couldn't bear to be seen

as one more terminal patient—opting instead
for permanent anesthesia. I seize
my pen, wondering what to write

to your children, who once were like siblings
to me: that love may not be enough
to save us? that despair

thinks only of itself
and should therefore be pitied? that privilege
is no cure for extinction?

How different your leave-taking
from this morning's more celebrated
casualty: Congressman John Lewis

who, departing amid his people's cries
of defiance, must have felt he was riding a wave
of change—the only antidote

to life's cancers. I imagine
your sons flying home
from Afghanistan, from Portland

(where the government's bungled crackdown
is sure to incite protest)
while I'm out walking the dog

in the late afternoon. Maybe like you
we've all felt a little abandoned
by God this year. A lone officer

on a motorcycle, strapped in his gear,
passes me at the corner and wheels around
to the curb for a serious chat

with his headset. Watching him
beneath leaden clouds, I begin to hear
a chant working its way up the street: "WHAT

do we WANT?" Tomorrow I will lie still
in corpse pose, thinking *I am but a witness*
to these restless impositions of body and mind,

but today? With the dog pulling his leash,
with a hot breeze
whapping the American flag like a parachute

outside the nursing home—signs everywhere
urging "Wash your hands"—
and demonstrators shouting

through surgical masks, I can only think
Something must be done!
And with a feeling almost

of deliverance, Mike, I give in
with tears of welcome
to a gusting wind.

Trench Art

It spoke to me across the cluttered shop
we'd wandered into. Slim and turtle brown,
the vase of hammered copper was inscribed
neatly in French—a single word, "Argonne,"
hinting at what it was. I picked it up
and recognized the shell-case underside.

The rheumy-eyed collector of antiques
grinned like a boy, and with a trembling hand
pointed to where the firing pin had tapped
and sprayed out leaden shrapnel seeds that fanned
the smoking fields. The delicate techniques
that soldiers learned to whittle their huge crop

of empty shells, inspired a kind of awe.
I saw them: young men desperate to go home
yet knowing war can't end until you win it.
They picked through scrap, believing there might come
from suffering, which all men undergo,
a trophy for one's shelf—with tulips in it.

Viking

He mucks the brickwork of his kiln
with slick, spreadable clay
to seal in heat.
All slag must burn away
for ore and charcoal to be fused
into crucible steel. The smelting, when complete,

yields him an ingot—glowing orange
between the forceps. Keen
to try its strength
and smooth any unforeseen
ripples in his material,
he pounds the sparking metal till its length

extends across the anvil. Hours
he hammers, each blow weighed
to bring a finer
tension to the blade.
He tapers her for pliancy,
bevels the hollow of her spine.

Now for the hand-cut alphabet
to inlay his best pledge.
Knowing the risk
of tampering with her edge,
he drives each iron letter home
with one shrill kiss.

Can she withstand a dunk in oil
to quench her newborn heat
(without that cursed
ping! signaling defeat

by some intrinsic flaw)? She can.
You've faced the worst,

he thinks, taking up a stone
to wipe away the scum
and watch the flame
of burnished metal come
like lightning inside her—
setting off his name.

Storm Windows

He pries back the wing clips, I pound on the frame
to jostle the wood from its paint-thickened trough.
"I got it," he mutters. Each May is the same.
Our system for taking the storm windows off

proceeds with a ladder: I hold it, he climbs;
as he cautiously lowers a pane of fogged glass,
I hand up a screen. We repeat seven times.
Although April was shitty (and March, a morass)

the north has backed off. Something shifts at the core.
We can sit on our porch with martinis tonight
and remark how a formerly bothersome chore
has evolved into some kind of marital rite.

In late fall we'll start over—we'll swap out the mesh
for the glass. To the sway of a nude maple bough
we'll sip scotch and watch firewood dwindle to ash,
then tuck under covers, unconscious of how

in our mud room, stationed against the wall,
is a rotating stockpile of screens or storms
to remind us of what we must reinstall
as our household climate cools or warms.

Black Ice

It forms in shadows: coldness no one sees
creeping through wintry rain or spring's first thaws
to lay its trap. It toys with physics' laws,
causing surface moisture to refreeze
so fast, a runner slips and cracks both knees
as Fate erupts in giggles of applause.
Reminded of life's undetected flaws,
the victim of its ambiguities
proceeds with caution. Spiritually bruised,
the fool no longer trusts his own two eyes
to find those spots where evil is confused
with good, where truth is lacquered slick with lies.
Instead he shuffles, trying to get used
to ground that gives way to a dark surprise.

You Scream I Scream

> "May the spirit of Actaeon move your heart."
> —Ovid's *Metamorphoses*

It was summer in Berkeley. I was 23,
sharing an attic loft my girlfriend rented
from a married couple: Harold, a young mechanic
and Jeannie, forty, who joked she was Harold's mom.
I'd take the bus home after Latin class
and, like a dutiful monk, translate Ovid
on a futon in our hot, cramped crawlspace.
It was quiet as a tomb. I didn't move
or make a sound, the day I heard keys thrown
on the kitchen table, something hollow smashing
against a wall. Soon I heard Jeannie scream
like no one ever had; it started low
and indecisive—rumbling in the throat
volcanically, then rising, note by note
into a shrill, possessed, *inhuman* sound.
To hear it seemed taboo. Like Actaeon
finding the goddess unclothed, I was afraid
of being discovered in my unholiness—
when Jeannie, with senses recovered, shouted up
our narrow stairwell. "Anybody there?"
I didn't want to answer, gulping back
the throb inside my heart, like hounded prey;
but hearing her foot touch the stairs, I cried
"I'm here." Crushed, Jeannie let out a sigh
and feeble laugh, saying I wasn't meant
to hear what I did. "I'm sorry, I'm sorry," I pled,
but what could we do, now that it was out—

that sonic boom of rage she knew I knew
had something to do with Harold's inadequacies?

Already on its way to me was a letter
from home, which I'd tear open days from now,
announcing my parents' divorce. It would burn my hand
where I lay on the futon, waiting to break the news
to Sally, the girl I hoped to marry one day.
That scream became a warning that engulfed us—
Harold, Jeannie, Mom, Dad, Sally, me—
with something like the final disappointment
of Ovid's hopefuls: howling as they turn
into a deer, a flower, a bird, a tree.

Saint Simone

She starved herself
thinking about grace.
How difficult it was

to be nothing
but flesh: prickly, contrarious,
pretending to get by

on cigarettes and headaches.
As a student, she witnessed
the heedless velocity

of factories; of campaigns
preparing to turn people
into things. She called this

force. Like any woman
who has loved a man,
she understood

God's absence—
the harrowing way
loss can intensify

passion. Denying herself
the comforts of church
or sect, she believed only

in challenge: staring
into the black waves
of oblivion

until they shimmered.

5. Beauty's Mark

1981

Can puberty inch toward us in a song?
For twelve weeks Sheena Easton's "Morning Train"
snakes up the charts—her banshee cry so strong,
its stab of bliss keeps rippling through my brain.
I hear it while I'm playing Centipede
at the roller rink. Through strobes of colored rain
I weave into the crowd and pick up speed,
noticing boys who take their girlfriends' hands—
the lather of their corduroy stampede
so musky with new fur and bulging glands.
A sophomore, gliding thoughtless as a swan,
hops and spins round to face me as he lands,
as though he's trying to pass me a baton.
O Sheena, does he know which track I'm on?

1983

I'm not prepared the first time Stevie Nicks
comes charging down the catwalk in "Stand Back"
with fan-blown curls—her dancers' Rockette kicks
proving how hard this muse of Fleetwood Mac
must hustle to command her own domain;
and singing, with the sadness of Eve's fall,
in a deep vibrato scalded by cocaine,
"He asked me for my love/ And that was all,"
she leads me to a life-enriching place
of reckoning—my sister self, the one
who sees behind this tearful, acned face
a need like hers—while I, the stricken son
tingle with pleasure, sensing in the dark
an exit wound where Beauty leaves its mark.

Out of the Labyrinth

> "Desire is a form of understanding."
> —From a review of David Thomson's *Sleeping with Strangers*

Somewhere between pretending and demanding,
you've managed to lose your way. Dropping the thread
that leads back to a civilizing fire,
you sense the darkened corridors expanding
behind you, adrenaline surging through your head.
This unrelenting problem of desire—
how to reconcile the beings you were
before and after leaving love's last bed—
encircles you: a quandary so entire
it keeps you up at night. Yet through the blur
of figures merged in groggy consciousness
come these words (charged with power to inspire
like an oracle) from a magazine you've read:
"Desire is a form of understanding."

Desire is a form of understanding?
You balk at first, sniffing it with suspicion.
Some hippie with a genius for rebranding
has blown dust off a New Age superstition—
the sort of feel-good mantra one can't bear.
Desire fills our minds with such hot air
we plot betrayals, fume like jealous bores,
read letters swiped from lovers' nightstand drawers
until our molten selfhood starts to quake.
Then, when the bliss for which we think we've strived
is ours? A staleness creeps into the cake.
Knowing how soon all passions are deprived
by being understood, you'd hate to make
the crude mistake of thinking you've arrived.

The crude mistake of thinking: you've arrived
at this very fork in the maze more than once.
Maybe the hippie's wise and you're the dunce
who's bypassed wisdom. Hasn't humanity thrived
by chasing nature's most alluring forms?
Plato thought that beauty was our model
for divine truth—and sober Aristotle
claimed all knowledge has its roots in yearning.
The systems mathematicians glean from swarms
of honeybees, suggest we'll go on learning
from the earth's sweetness. Hearing a mockingbird
run through its meadow trills, you feel complete—
a child again, laughing as if you've heard
lovely words you're nervous to repeat.

Lovely words you're nervous to repeat
have dogged your every step. Trying to forget
a princess you left dangling far from Crete,
you've lain awake and watched the bachelorette
evolve into a diadem of stars.
She's ruled your puny freedom with the force
of a goddess—Venus dominating Mars
long after their dishonored intercourse.
It's hard to put in words, that first love's truth.
You still hold back (when students ask today
whether the ancient Greeks were really gay)
the unheroic story of your youth—
its wholesome fruit, how men like you were wived
in paradise, where Satan first contrived.

In paradise, where Satan first contrived
temptation, unpicked apples gleamed like gods.
Sampling their flesh, you thought you'd beat the odds
against a thrilling life—though what survived
were merely reenactments of that dream.
No fruit, however ripe, could quite restore
your faith in love's replenishing esteem.
One chewed and chewed, yet never reached the core
of beauty. Pink light fills a Western sky
tonight; you hum a verse from an old song—
"Great temptations never really die"—
and tear your cured bacon in two. How strong
the appetite, you think—how bittersweet
the knowledge that consumes us as we eat.

The knowledge that consumes us, as we eat
through each new layer of nature's loveliness,
is that we'll go on feeling incomplete
yet won't seek out adventure any less.
Even the grimmest soldier, sage, or saint
can't nullify desire with restraint.
Most men behave like Ithacans at last:
insisting someone tie them to a mast
just so they'll know what sin they're giving up.
A poet's different. He dives in and plays,
while others mind the oarlocks of their schooling,
until his task appears—beyond all fooling—
and sets out to refill his battered cup
with a diviner judgment: lovers' praise.

With a diviner judgment, lovers praise
the ardent youth who seeks out shapely forms—
who looks into a fellow swimmer's gaze
and reads the lightning etched in thunderstorms.
No April bloom could be too aromatic,
no wood too dense, no garden too erratic
or dance too wild for one whose body warms
with every draft of summer's sparkling wine.
But you? You've picked up too much moral static.
The tune's grown faint; your whiskers taste of brine.
There's one last stitch of hope left undefiled:
if only, before you cross life's finish line,
you solve this maze—set free the shackled child
and let him live—you'll grasp the whole design.

And let him live! You'll grasp the whole; design
a future in which no youth is sacrificed
to depths of Shame. This convoluted shrine
laid open, crowds will queue up in the sun
declaring, though admission is overpriced,
it moves them to imagine what you've done.
But that's years off. There's still an Antichrist
to be destroyed. Now that you've reached the center
of love's black basement, you've only begun
to face the actual foe. Go on, reenter
the sanctum of desire's outcast son.
There, in the murk of torchlit passageways,
whose mirrored walls reflect a smoky haze,
you'll find the monster groping through the maze.

You'll find the monster, groping through the maze
with nostrils flared: a connoisseur of maleness.
Height, gait, girth, weight, hairiness or paleness
inhaled by eyes that measure as they graze,
he waits in nooks for gymnasts of Achaea
to strip for sport. Nor does he think it odd
this beauty he pursues is a façade:
an outline only, not the lived idea
of manhood. How could centuries of survival
have brought him here?—to circle an abyss;
to skulk in corners waiting for the kiss
of transformation—waiting for a rival
to drive him squealing like a lassoed swine
from underworlds where bodies intertwine.

From underworlds where bodies intertwine
it's hard to look away, but you will do it.
In every quest, a spark of the divine
(or fear of what might happen if we blew it)
steadies us as we pass each open door.
By stepping through, you may wind up regretting
the aim of your desire was nothing more
than change—of plot, theme, character, or setting.
Change is what mythologies are for:
the moonlight one demands in this nocturne
called life. And then? A glimmering at dawn—
an outbreak of applause as you discern
the maze's entrance—all this darkness gone
in time for celebration. You'll return

in time for celebration—you'll return
as guest of honor at your best friend's wedding!
Surprised to find out that's where you were heading
(since happiness is something people earn
or stumble into with beginner's luck),
you toast the groom, indulge in petit fours
and tiered cake (topped with . . . little minotaurs?)
and stride across the dancefloor. Horrorstruck
to see you're nude waist-down, you wake up screaming:
this whole time you've been in the labyrinth, dreaming
like Dorothy in Kansas. Just like her,
you're desperate to rejoin the human pack.
Why dawdle here—your own self-saboteur?
Accept the hope of finding your way back.

Except the hope of finding your way back
means getting used to life in black and white.
You've been desire's monomaniac
so long, what's wrong has started to feel right.
Won't you miss the daily firefight—
this war between the conscience and the senses?
If there's a road to peace, it's out of sight;
desire will trigger all your old defenses.
You're doomed to be its simmering volcano—
its Oedipus, whom longing left so lonely
he pierced his eyes (the ultimate "Just say no").
Who looks to spring's new crop, desiring only
what he has? Or smells the flowers, unconcerned,
without forgetting everything you've learned?

Without forgetting, everything you've learned
would stall the quests of braver men than you.
Perhaps it's best some corners are not turned.
Beauty survives, a beast we can't subdue:
the svelte black stallion bursting from the barn
to lure one more sad cowboy to his end.
Hey! What's that—on the ground, around the bend?
Frayed wool? Is it . . . the princess's drawn-out yarn!
Tail end of the tethering you left.
Its clipped braid signals what you know is true:
desire will be your only almanac
to wiser husbandry. Why live bereft
forever? Come on, you know you're dying to
pick up the thread, reverse the winding track.

Pick up the thread; reverse the winding track
without forgetting everything you've learned.
Accept the hope of finding your way back
in time for celebration. You'll return
from underworlds where bodies intertwine;
you'll find the monster groping through the maze
and let him live. You'll grasp the whole design
with a diviner judgment. Lovers praise
the knowledge that consumes us as we eat
in paradise, where Satan first contrived
lovely words. You're nervous to repeat
the crude mistake of thinking you've arrived.
Desire is a form of understanding
somewhere between pretending and demanding.

Sappho at the Beach

Slick with lotion, bellies of women dozing
swell and sink. The palms of their feet find coolness
burrowing in sand. As a draft of pooled heat
nibbles the ocean,

Zoë turns to me with her burnished body.
"Let's clean up," she snuffles, "and get some dinner."
Always famished, this one. I pass her sweet grapes,
watching her seize one

nimbly in her teeth and detach it. Crushing
juice from flesh, she closes her eyes and praises
Earth for grapes and beautiful women. "Itch!" she
squeals, so I scratch it—

buttered skin, too teased where the curl of ringlets
grazes neck and back. On a whim I press her,
"How about a swim?" For I've spied another
Nereid easing

hips through sea foam, wading to deeper water.
Goddess, what unrest are you contemplating?
Off she goes: head plunging, then bobbing up for
air, as a poem

breathes itself afloat. A momentum takes her
farther out than planned, where she gathers ocean
into outstretched arms—and with swoops of cupped hands
splashes her bosom.

Zoë, clucking, signals her disapproval.
Beauty's hex has waylaid me once again: drugged
reason, disarmed pride—while my heart, in pieces,
clings to the orchid

of some witch of sex for its bold labellum.
Goddess, help me! Guide me toward your secret
wisdom, sealed in coconut-scented creases
softer than vellum.

William Shakespeare

a lipogram after Mark Zimmerman

As Will, I am small: a simple lease maker,
ill speller, arse slapper, serial liar;

while as Hal, Lear, Emilia, I am ample, wise—
imperial as a sapphire.

A peeress's warm whispers? Praise? A male heir?
Please! We mammals shall wail similar wishes

while eras pass, harmless. Same hammer, same mark.
Malaise wears a sham smile, like a rapier

whereas I seek real war. I skewer similes
as a shark samples his kill. I milk phrases, relish

whimsies, release Hell's seraphim like Raphael
as he smears his easel. A mask-realm's Ariel,

I raise paper messiahs, shape karma's laws.
Where else shall we see, hear, smell

a merrier empire? Ma'am, Sir, I swear: we are all
sleepwalkers, mere hemispheres, semi-aware.

What He Saw in the River

A pumpkin: floating, opening underneath
like a peplum skirt. Hopelessly waterlogged,
it let the current lap its navel pleat
and nudge it to shore. Through frayed clouds, sunset
burnished the rind a Chinese-lantern orange.
It glowed inside the skyline's mirrored blues,
drawing his eye toward the deeper murk

on which it floated: cold black tea
infused with moiled silt, with gasoline
from tugs and cruisers. Crossing his forearms,
he leaned against the railing to observe
the rumpled husk—revolving like a moon
above an uninhabitable canyon—
and thought of how the mind makes what it sees

a sort of hub around which all else turns.
Monstrous garbage, punted with fatigue
at the very holiday it represented
(as if its hanging on might anchor time
too firmly), its ennui reminded him
of what one keeps forgetting. Weightlessness
is always nature's underlying state.

Shaping his lips around the word "November,"
he felt time slip for a moment from its tether
as nightlamps along the walkway flickered on.
He watched the pumpkin drift and disappear
into reflections—like a sun's dissolve—
where shadows widened and a drawbridge spanned
the current, churning coins of fiery light.

Tree Swallows

Leaving their nests to feed and fly and play,
    the swallows begin
        hovering over the river at midday:
    white bibs with black wings, weaving in
and out of one another's wakes, they call dibs
    on mayflies as they graze
        leafing willows, glide and swoop
    upward in a corkscrew loop-de-loop
to an aerial summit, where they pivot
    into a death-defying plummet
        toward their shadows in the dappled water.
    Back and forth, they flit and tease;
frisky tacticians—no warier
    than fighter pilots scrimmaging
        in formation above an aircraft carrier
    weeks from a mission.
You love to watch the scamps
    mount pretend attacks, as you wait
        for a precious, flyby glimpse
    of the turquoise on their backs.

Those streaks of blue!—those sequins
    glinting like abalone shells
        embroidered in coat tails;
    those dragonfly neckties
skimming the surface of the afternoon
    with skipped-stone frequencies;
        sound waves
    splashing one's body
in the *plink* of piano keys; coruscations
    like knife throws—minnows fleeing
        from cavernous reefs. *To swallow
    and be swallowed:* oh, how

this planet has made us
    idiots for beauty! Pawns and purveyors
        of aesthetic (if not artistic)
    accidents of mutation, we fall behind

in making of the swallows'
    half-balletic, half-ballistic
        circus routine, a tune
    or dance—a mural, a romance
of language linking mind to mind. Is this
    why, hours from now,
        you'll sit in a chair
    and stare at a desktop screen, repeatedly
asking, *Is this? Is this what I mean?* Too aware
    of the danger (while people live at odds
        in the rising smoke
    of half-extinguished gods)
you'll create through the night:
    feeling your way
        to a river where even the blind might see
    the passerine
advancing, tree by tree.

Natural Wonder

I am arterial
surge, unstoppable
carbon exhaust
gusting through bronchial
branches. I am
winter's filter—
steady exchange
of moisture and heat
through pores,
sensation's chain
reactor, a spinal
telecom, conductor
of impulse
down a nervous
lace of extremities.
I am a hotbed
of microbes,
minutely capillaried
nest of salts
and hormone
concentrates. I am
seed expelled
from a gland,
salivary ooze
of enzyme and antibody,
mucal glaze
of membranes,
toughened cartilage
and bone. I am
a boweled extractor
of minerals,
a 24-hour cellular

superfactory
recharging in sleep.
I am Earth's
fantasist: photosensitive
rod-and-cone
perceiver of rainbows
through mist, synaptic
brainfold conceiver
of godhood, gushing
at sunset: *Just look
at Nature!
Isn't she beautiful?*

6. Queer Physics

1983

I flip through *Newsweek,* stopping at an ad
in which an oiled Adonis trains his pecs
on a home gym. "Body by Soloflex":
the invitation to a workout fad
kindles my envy. Transfixed, I see
in the bronzed and airbrushed California dude
a statue come to life—a svelte Greek nude
who's practically the opposite of me.
Envy begins to melt into desire
as contoured navel, nipples, shoulders, chin
brand me with their perfection. I perspire,
leaving a thumbprint smudge of salty black.
Dry-mouthed as Lot's wife, I am taking in
a view from which I never can turn back.

1984

I'm pear-shaped, pimpled, sedentary, shy:
a teenage Quasimodo awed by cliques.
Raising a fist at destiny, I buy
a book called *Working Out* by Charles Hix.
I learn how to build muscle and burn fat
from ham-thighed men in Speedos—sinewed, stocky—
whose dumbbell repetitions on a mat
become my inspiration. Grim as Rocky
I lunge and lift and curl and crunch my abs,
work up a sweat on bike treks, eat low-cal,
and go to bed ignoring hunger's stabs—
till one day, in the mirror, my morale
shifts with a glimpse of masculinity
that any stranger might mistake for me.

1985

A school day, cool yet mild. I stay home sick.
A lawn chair on our screened-in patio
ferries me to Long Island, where, like Nick,
I fall for Gatsby's charms. Words form slow
trains through a fog of antihistamines;
in stages I can barely comprehend,
a young man's passion quickens and careens
with absurd hope toward its violent end.
I look up now and then, watching the sun
chase shadows from our curled banana leaves;
I doze off; pour some Coke. When Nick is done
hallowing Gatsby's dream, my whole chest heaves:
never have I felt the distant past
sink this deep, in a quietude this vast.

Notes Toward a Queer Physics

quantum bits:
the either/and/or

particles of being
instantly transmitted

across space—
attraction's valences

revealed only
when observed

LGBTQIA +
encryptions

too deep to hack:
the anywhere

between M and F,
the Mother Father

God please quit
asking what

I am other than
estranged

and stranded,
your splintered

lover
eternally

seeking/avoiding
entanglement

Staying at Dad's

Picture a house so quiet, you hear time
    absorbing each day's measure of the sun,
and through French doors, the tinkling of a chime
    (to indicate that happy hour's begun)
links day to day, to week, to month, to year.
    Now ask yourself, *How long have I been here?*

Neighbors carrying cocktails walk their dogs
    on retractable leads, while round the cul-de-sac
a ten-year-old in training blithely jogs.
    You sit in the driveway, watching squirrels snack
on birdfeed meant for woodpeckers and doves
    to fortify their hurried, hungry loves.

Out back, a filter roams the burbling pool.
    Beyond Dad's lot, a steel-wire cattle fence
tempts cows to wedge their heads through barbs—and drool
    into his birdbath font some common sense.
Their shrubby field, hemmed in by pine and palm,
    cushions the freeway's roar. That keeps Dad calm.

Come in. This shrine of white and cream and bone,
    whose lofted ceilings store forgotten prayers,
is tranquil—save for the infrequent tone
    of casters on the wicker dining chairs
rumbling across stone tile. In rainy weather,
    a jigsaw puzzle slowly comes together

on Carol's tabletop, while Dad reclines
    to watch the news, his finger poised on MUTE.
At four, she'll crack the ice; he'll pour their wines;
    they'll raise a toast to show how resolute
the leisures of retirement can be.
    Heroic, almost. Have a glass; you'll see.

A 20th-Century Scrapbook

Amelia Earhart
  seizing the controls;

Stephen Hawking
  fathoming black holes;

Jackson Pollock
  letting pigment spill;

Oppenheimer
  sundering God's will;

Rachel Carson
  charting birth defects;

Malcolm Little
  renaming himself X;

Alan Turing
  neutered, life's work stalled;

Elie Wiesel
  inside Buchenwald;

Che Guevara
  tallying men's worth;

Neil Armstrong
  welling up at little Earth.

When knowledge turns
  to dust, we feel our skin

grow hotter, damp, electric.
   Truth sinks in.

Ghost Tour

1

December in Savannah. Freezing hands
hold sensors whose red lights begin to spark.
Our tour guide, with his fingertips, expands
an iPad photo (granular and dark)
of a white-shawled specter brooding on a porch.
We'd hoped his ghost tales might relight a torch
of the old South interred in crumbling brick—
not bore us with this paranormal schtick.

2

We rise at eight from our four-poster bed,
sip tea while soaking up the inn's décor,
descend the staircase—ready to be fed.
Sensing our presence through the kitchen door,
a Black cook comes with biscuits and a knife.
Before our eyes, the South's ghosts pulse with life.

The Pelican

Let me fly serenely
    above the silver bay,
        no rival birds between me
    and a deep, elusive prey.

Let there be no distractions
    when, following the course
        of myriad refractions,
    I stalk their moving source.

Then let me wheel in silence
    on my angelic span.
        With concentrated violence,
    let me fold my fan

and dive without detection
    toward a silver meal—
        piercing my reflection
    to feed upon the real.

Laughing with Alice

Hearing the news that she'd died,
I suddenly remembered
how Alice and I once served
on the same hiring committee;
how, during a phone interview,
the pretentious cadence
and fluted nasal vowels
of an Ivy League applicant
pricked us with such an acute
sense of the ridiculous,
our eyes met over a tremor
of giggles. Impossible
to stifle—with that voice
droning away, its owner
so solemn, so oblivious
to a giddiness now taking hold
of everyone at the table—
our mad laughter grew.
The harder we struggled
to plug it with the backs of our hands
or dodge each other's
incriminating gaze, the more
our eyes filled with tears.
Helplessly we tried to wave
away the contagion, each word
from the speakerphone
like a needle to the spine,
convulsing us—until,
with a smothered gasp and sob
and complete seizure
of the abdomen, we passed
into that final phase

of ecstasy: a rictus
like a cat's yawn, the soul unable
to claw its way back
into the paralyzed body.
Somehow Alice, though still high
on hilarity's ether,
pulled herself together
in time to say goodbye
on behalf of the committee,
as we found our breath again
and dabbed our eyes.

An Aging Poet Explains

The problem is that people are like trees.
Although they think and speak and walk around,
they're growths of buried systems no one sees—
whose roots, like an inverted broccoli crown,
anchor them to the soils of home and school.
While summer wraps their limbs in gathered light,
this hidden half digests a springtime pain
that hardens them, with long-forgotten rain.
The next time someone rankles you? Don't fight:
picture them standing mirrored by a pool,
such that the branching of their inborn fire
appears as this root self, grown upside down—
and watch the seasoned bully, cheat, or liar
become a child trying not to drown.

Ferns

Each spring, their spiral heads
   protrude from dampened soil
like shepherds' crooks. As leaf by leaf
   their sprouting fronds uncoil,

young ferns take their destined shape.
   Fringed feathers, brightly splayed
and sprinkled with the April dew,
   fan open in the shade—

except for the very tips,
   whose last leaves hold their curl
like little fists, as though refusing
   ever to unfurl.

Then comes a sunny afternoon
   when, starting to get warm
with hoarded dreams, the curled hands stretch
   to grace the air with form.

Love Keeps Coming

From windows left open;
from text-message screens
and moms eating hot fudge sundaes;
from warmed-up jeans
flopping out of the dryer;
from the ink-and-cabernet stains
of winter sunsets; from the not-yet-broken
silence just before a kiss:
little by little, from that, from this,
love keeps coming.

Sometimes it floats
on a thank-you note,
or in the walnut eyes
of a checkout clerk. Sometimes it flickers
in the headlights
of a driver letting you in—or flirts
with the raciness of a late-night
L.A. comedian.
From the creased sleeves of Christmas shirts
unfolded pin by pin,
love keeps coming.

It's bubbling up: from teenage musicians,
artists, teachers, program directors,
gamers and gardeners, cops and beauticians,
sports fans and beach bums
digging it out of the ground
with metal detectors.
Even the dog tracks it in
on wet paws, gnawing a bone,

wearing an idiotic grin.
The thunderous drums
of applause for a quarterback's
pass to the end zone; the tender hands
of volunteer caregivers; the courage
of deathbed physicians
reminds us
how love keeps coming.

It can't be stopped. It's crossing
borders, scrambling signals,
rounding up captives and taking no orders
from politicians. The signs, plain to see
as neon lights
on a theater marquee
or the faces of friends in the street,
are not to be feared; there's nothing scary
about the pale orange glaze
of sunlight on last night's snowfall
in the cemetery,
or the white whiskers marbling your beard,
or the workday swallowed at seven
with a bourbon sting,
when love keeps coming

and the first forsythias of spring
break out in papery fire
against a parking lot fence.
One cardinal sings
and presto: your whistling grandad,
the king of common sense,

comes back to life, a bridegroom
garlanded with lilacs, to warn you, *Look out*
for all this love—in flannel sheets
and deerskin caps, the petrichor
of rain-washed streets,
the ordure of fields, smell of sycamores
and coffee shops. From used record stores,
from rest stops on highways,
from supper-club cocktails,
gulf seas and blue skies
and the knowing depths of your favorite eyes
to look into,
love keeps coming.

About the Author

David Southward grew up in southwest Florida and earned degrees in English from Northwestern and Yale Universities. Since 1998 he has taught literature and graphic arts in the Honors College at the University of Wisconsin-Milwaukee.

David's poetry collections include *Bachelor's Buttons* (Kelsay Books, 2020) and *Apocrypha,* a sonnet sequence based on the Gospels (Wipf & Stock, 2018). He is a two-time winner of the Lorine Niedecker Prize from the Council for Wisconsin Writers, and in 2019 his poem "Mary's Visit" received the Frost Farm Prize for Metrical Poetry. David resides in Milwaukee with his husband, Geoff, and their two beagles.

Read more at:
davidsouthward.com

www.ingramcontent.com/pod-product-compliance
Lightning Source LLC
Chambersburg PA
CBHW022142160426
43197CB00009B/1398